Exploring America Series

Alabama - Travelogue by State

Experience Both the Ordinary and Obscure

By Amber Richards

Table of Contents

Introduction

In this series, we'll be taking a look, at one American state at a time to explore. In this book, we'll be looking at the beautiful state of Alabama.

Whether you are a resident of Alabama, or plan to visit, we'll be checking out cool places to see and interesting things to do. Some of these will be well known, popular options, while others will be more obscure, out of the way places to discover.

This was written in collaboration with a resident of Alabama, to offer a local's perspective of the area. Often times that offers a completely different view of an area, than when written by a travel guide.

The focus of this series is not about where to stay and eat (unless that offers a truly unique experience for the region), but about the towns, the local life, nature, landscape, some history, and things to do while in Alabama. You will also find chapters on ghost towns, popular fairs & festivals to take in, and family friendly things to do.

Alabama - Famous For

Alabama the Beautiful attracts more than 20 million tourists annually, but what is it that makes Alabama so beautiful? Perhaps it's our tens of thousands of miles of rivers and streams, which are home to endangered species and fishermen alike. Some say it's our vastly different landscapes, allowing one to climb a mountain, go spelunking (caving), and relax on a white sand beach, all in the same weekend. Others believe it's our history, beautifully haunted by Dr. Martin Luther King's "Letter from Birmingham Jail."

It could be argued that one of the most beautiful parts of Alabama isn't just what can be seen, but what can be experienced. A sunset over an ancient Indian ceremonial ground after fishing in the Crappie Capital of the world makes a day that will grace your memories for a lifetime. A riverside southern rock music experience will likely leave lyrics in your head for weeks, so much so that, if you are here for summer, you just might stick around for another dose. If Alabama is the first southern state you visit, you'll likely be so charmed by the southern hospitality that you'll grab a tall glass of sweet tea and stay a while. I reckon you "oughta."

In its tangled past, Alabama has been known as the birthplace of Helen Keller, the Heart of Dixie, the central locale for the civil rights movement, and the cotton state. In its present, it is known for its Magic City, NASA and the U.S. Space and Rocket Center, white sand beaches that boast being some of the cleanest in the country, and some of the nation's best breweries, which continue to win national awards.

Though part of its past is a bit dark – particularly when it fell central to the civil rights movement during the governance of George Wallace – Alabama has done a fantastic job of embracing its history front and center, in the midst of its revitalization. Most importantly, it may be the only state one ever visits where the tea is just as sweet as the locals.

Years ago, visitors to the state saw a much different picture than the one painted for us today. Monuments are still spread from north to south in Alabama, in order to commemorate the "cotton state days," the Trail of Tears, the Civil War, and the Civil Rights Movement.

Of course, a trip to Alabama shouldn't be all about the past. Presently, the state is a natural haven for fishermen, campers, and lovers of nature alike, and even has quite its share of entertainment phenomena. From the recording sensations that occur in Muscle Shoals, to one of the nation's most difficult race car tracks at Talladega, one is sure to find entertainment around every corner.

There are countless things for which Alabama could be known, and depending on whom you stop to ask, you may very well receive a hundred different answers. However, one thing is certain: When it comes to locals, we usually tend to think that everything leads back to the water.

Upper Caney Creek Falls in the William B

Bankhead National Forest of Alabama

Excluding our shoreline, we have almost half a million

acres of rivers, streams, ponds, lakes, and bays. The first word

Helen Keller is thought to have comprehended was spelled

into Anne Sullivan's hand as "w-a-t-e-r," as the pump water rushed onto their hands in Colbert County, where her birthplace and the same well pump remains.

Water is central to almost everything the locals enjoy. Perhaps it is the way one looks past the hot summers, for which the state is undoubtedly known. In fact, if one is willing to trust the methods of the locals, he or she would find that there is amazing music to be both discovered and enjoyed along the waters.

In the Heart of Dixie, you'll find that music is a backdrop for everything in the summertime. From Gulf Shore's Hangout Music Festival, all the way north to Gadsden's annual Riverfest, you'll find it difficult to decide whether to spend the days discovering a new blues band in a

Jazz pub, or taking a road trip to Muscle Shoals, where the voices of Aretha Franklin, Elvis Presley, and Lynyrd Skynyrd still echo through the waters.

This part of Alabama's culture is so deeply instilled that even segregation and civil rights protests didn't stop the creation of the some of the most legendary historical "soul" recordings performed among divided races with the bands in Muscle Shoals. In an era when the entire nation seemed black and white, the music remained soulful and colorblind. Some say it was just "something in the water."

Of course, whether or not locals are cooling off in the water, they're certain to discuss one thing the state is known for nationwide – its college football rivalry between Auburn University and the University of Alabama.

The rivalry is the one thing that turns the sweet tea attitudes to pure sour ones. It has run pure since 1948, and if your tourist plans in Alabama ever encourage you to call the state home, you'll be forced to choose a side, even if you hate football, because after all, your mother or grandfather at some point enjoyed the sport, and you may as well choose now, before you're adopted into the wrong team in the midst of an ugly Iron Bowl.

Just in case you think the rivalry is overrated, consider the following: the rivalry between the two sides was so intense after one of the first Iron Bowls ended in a tie that from 1907 to 1948, the teams could not set aside differences long enough to compete against each other again. In 1947, the Alabama House of Representatives interfered to help restart the competition we all know today.

The games began being played at Legion Field, which is where the name of the match up originates (Legion Field is located in Birmingham, famous for its iron production). The Iron Bowl would be moved from Legion Field decades later, in part due to its seemingly shrinking capacity in comparison to its fan base.

Birmingham, Alabama Skyline

If you aren't drawn in by football but still love other

sports, there are also minor league baseball teams in

Montgomery, Huntsville, and the state's largest city –

Birmingham (a.k.a., the "Magic City"). In fact, the new home

field of the Birmingham Barons – Region's Field – was voted

Ballpark of the Year in 2013. Though the Barons originally

played downtown in the 1880's, they spent decades afterward

playing in the city's suburbs, returning "home" in 2013.

This phenomenal park offers outstanding views of the

Magic City skyline, all while being situated between the

famous Railroad Park and world renowned research

powerhouse, The University of Alabama at Birmingham. In

fact, UAB and the medical district may even be seen from the

Baron's third base side.

The spectacular opportunities for seeing a Magic City

sunset certainly do not stop at Region's Field. Any visitor of the Magic City should visit the Vulcan, second only to the statue of liberty as the tallest metal statue in the nation. The views atop the observation deck feature Region's Field and beyond.

Hiking trails beneath the Roman statue are sure to satisfy city and nature lovers alike. In the days of Greek mythology, the Roman god of forge (a furnace used to heat and shape metal) was Vulcan. The statue of this Roman god overlooks the very area of Birmingham that provided the materials for the iron and steel creation that built the Magic City.

The Vulcan statue, though much different in appearance now than upon its arrival to the city in 1905, arrived during a very controversial time in Alabama. Alabama

had only been readmitted to the Union for a mere 37 years,

nurturing the generation that lost over 25,000 state residents'

lives in the Civil War.

During this time, U.S. Steel had just purchased

Birmingham's Tennessee Coal, Iron, and Railroad Co., and

most of those who had lost their land, or had become heavily

indebted during the war, were forced to work long hours in

cotton mills. Locals experienced heavy unrest, and a major

political shift began to happen. Suddenly, almost all blacks

and poor whites found themselves unable to vote, and the Jim

Crow laws were just over the horizon.

Though amendments were added to the constitution

regarding the freedom of slaves and the right to vote decades prior, the South continued to press for fewer and fewer rights of blacks. For example, one law in Birmingham clearly stated, "It shall be unlawful for a negro and white person to play together, or in company with each other, at any game of pool or billiards."

White nurses were not required to practice in wards that housed blacks. Railroads and buses had regulations regarding where blacks could sit – or even simply wait – on a train or bus. The segregation of transportation, along with laws that prevented blacks and whites from eating at the same restaurant (unless there were specifically separate doors to enter), were two of the most heavily protested laws. Even toilet facilities and drinking water fountains were segregated.

During the 1950's, there began to be a change on the

horizon. Uprisings were happening throughout the South, but Birmingham was quickly moving to center stage. Shortly afterward, the movement called "The Birmingham Campaign" began marches and protests downtown.

Through their perseverance, change began to slowly happen. Signs were removed that specified "Blacks Only" or "Whites Only" in 1963. However, just a few short months later, four girls were killed in the bombing of Sixteenth Street Baptist Church, an event which was organized by segregationists. This is only one of 18 unsolved bombings thought to be carried out by segregationists.

On April 12, 1963 (Good Friday), Dr. Martin Luther King, Jr. had chosen Birmingham as the focal point for his campaign, and he had decided to add himself to the list of overcrowded jailhouse residents. Here, King wrote "Letter from Birmingham Jail," using pieces of newspaper, bath tissue, and a pencil.

King was released days later, and local protestors began using children to march for their cause. After all, children had fewer responsibilities and there was an incorrect assumption that they would not be jailed. Nearly 1,000 were arrested in the city over the course of one peaceful protest event. The following day, more children arrived at Kelly Ingram Park and were met with high pressure fire hoses, which sent them tumbling down into the street.

Fortunately, President Kennedy's eyes were watching as the nation gasped in horror, and a civil rights bill was finally proposed. A quarter million people of all races gathered for support, and the famous "I Have a Dream" speech was delivered by King in Washington, D.C., on that day.

One could spend an entire day visiting all of the civil rights attractions in the city of Birmingham alone. Sixteenth Street Baptist Church may be seen in the background of Kelly Ingram Park, and the city of Birmingham has dedicated an entire district to Alabama Civil Rights. The city has one of the nation's best Civil Rights Institutes, where segregated water fountains may still be seen today. Here, haunting side-by-side comparisons may be seen among the classrooms for whites and blacks, with astounding differences. A replica of the Freedom Rider bus is also held at the institute, along with the actual armored police vehicles that were used to attack protestors.

The institute is situated between the neighborhood blocks where the protests and arrests took place, and is across the street from Sixteenth Street Baptist Church, which was recently nominated as a UNESCO World Heritage Site. The institute's president, as if to provide a sign of just how much progress has been made, was chosen as the state's tourism professional of the year.

It didn't take long after the civil rights movement for Alabama to begin quickly accelerating forward. Over a decade prior to King's "I have a Dream" speech, the Redstone Arsenal in Huntsville was busy working with hundreds of rocket scientists. In 1958, America's first orbiting satellite was launched. Only two years later, a team at the arsenal would develop rockets for a lunar landing, and in 1960, the

Marshall Space Flight Center was officially activated.

Shortly thereafter, the United States launched its first astronaut into space (upon visiting the Marshall Flight Center, one can still see the test sand from Alan B. Shepard's flight.). President Kennedy then presented a challenge: The nation would land an astronaut on the moon and safely return him, before 1970.

The Marshall Center provided six rockets that were used for this purpose, as well as developed a roving vehicle for the astronauts' transportation after they landed on the moon. An immense amount of research is still completed at the NASA Marshall Space Flight Center, now a National Historic Landmark.

Nearby, the United States Space and Rocket Center provides a fascinating look into this frontier with both historical artifacts and modern day science attractions. While preparing to send astronauts to the moon, Dr. Wernher von Braun also made a proposition to the Alabama Legislature for a permanent museum. After votes were cast, the U.S. Army donated part of the Redstone Arsenal for the site of the museum, which would be on the same site as the NASA center.

The museum now displays tens of millions of dollars in hardware, including the nation's first satellite, as well as more recent and current hardware. It hosts a Space Camp, simulations, and other interactive activities for people all ages, and it is also home to a space dome and more. Among paid tourism destinations, The Space and Rocket Center was

Alabama's most visited in 2013.

In summary, Alabama is known for its rich history, with remnants displayed in museums and even along roadsides. The state is also known for its world renowned research at the University of Alabama at Birmingham, as well as the sites that encompass what once was (and still is) the Magic City. It is known for the rich, soulful sounds that echo from the waters of Muscle Shoals, as well as for overcoming the Civil Rights movement and rising up to become a revitalized, beautiful, soulful haven for music lovers, outdoor enthusiasts, fans of intense sports rivalries, white sand beaches, Mardi Gras and some of the best-hidden treasures of soul-food the south may ever see. Furthermore, perhaps most fascinating of all is in the background for which all of the state is known: it boasts being the only state in the nation that is home to both the best doctors in the nation and some of the

best rocket scientists worldwide.

Parks in Alabama

DeSoto Caverns and Amusement Park

Southeast of Birmingham lies DeSoto Caverns and Amusement Park. The main cavern room is 120 feet high and has been known to Native Americans for thousands of years. In fact, the oldest cave graffiti in the nation may be found here. Centuries after the cave drawings were made, the caverns were used to supply gun powder manufacturing materials during the Civil War.

Its history doesn't end there, however, as it was also a speakeasy (where alcohol was illegally sold during the prohibition). However, this effort failed after several shootings ensued, and it was closed by federal agents. Bullet holes may still be seen today inside the cavern. More fascinating, however, is that the cavern is one of few places in which one can experience "total darkness."

The cavern site features an amusement park that is primarily focused on children, or those who are young at heart. Towering forts provide the perfect battleground for a water balloon tossing war. There are also gem panning activities, a giant hamster wheel, trail mazes, a train that tours the park, and more.

Cathedral Caverns

Located between Grant and Woodville, Cathedral Caverns is less than three hours away from Desoto Caverns Family Fun Park, and they could be an amazing part of a vacation entirely centered on caverns! The cave has been opened to the public (with a brief closing) since 1955. When the original owner's wife first entered the cave, its grand entrance sparked her to describe it as a "cathedral." Now a 461 acre national park, it is known as Cathedral Caverns.

The grand entrance that inspired the cavern's name is 25 feet tall and 126 feet wide, making it the widest entrance to any cave in the world. There is a frozen waterfall inside of the caverns, as well as the largest stalagmite in the world, which reaches 45 feet high. The cave stays around 60 degrees year round, so it's perfect to visit any time of the year.

Not only does the cave break multiple world records, but legends say that the cave can even predict the weather via a cloud that sometimes seeps out of the mouth of the cave. Generally, when this cloud is seen, rain arrives within 48 hours. Artifacts from the cave date back as far as 9000 years ago, indicating the presence of Native Americans with arrowheads, pottery remnants, and evidence of fire pits.

DeSoto State Park and Little River

Named after Hernando De Soto, DeSoto State Park is located near Mentone, Alabama. It features a waterfall that is 104 feet tall, which empties into the Little River. The park encompasses over three thousand acres and has a variety of lodging, from chalets to campgrounds. The Little River and the area that surrounds it provide an abundance of activities for nature lovers. There are over 25 miles of trails (mountain bikes are welcome), as well as kayaking, skiing, bouldering, propelling, and more.

This area's landscape is noticeably different from that of southern Alabama. The Mentone area proves that, regardless whether you are looking for a beach or a mountain town, all you need is a visit to Alabama.

Little River Canyon National Preserve is another astonishing part of Alabama's canyons. Near Fort Payne, the canyon begins with a giant, 45 foot waterfall. During winter and spring, water levels are high enough for kayaks, and in the summer, they provide an excellent place to escape the Alabama heat. There is an abundance of parking for RVs on site, although camping is not permitted in the waterfall area. The beautiful Little River is often compared to Yellowstone River canyon, with cliffs as high as 600 feet above the river.

It is considered one of Alabama's ten Natural Wonders and, like Yellowstone, is even home to rainbow trout. The river has the potential to be a skilled fisherman's haven, being home to over four types of bass, as well as bream and catfish.

However, the beauty of Little River is actually an obstacle for fishermen.

The crystal clear water makes it difficult to catch during typical fishing conditions, so one must fish when the light is low, or after a rain. It should also be noted that bait should be chosen carefully for this region, since the fish in Little River are small-mouthed.

The area of Little River is large, and there are many entrances among two counties, so it is important to decide which area of the river to visit before entering. National Park Service Maps can provide helpful insight for fishermen looking to find the best entrance for a good catch.

Regardless of the entrance chosen, there are plenty of

breathtaking views and access to a variety of outdoor activities (even hunting is allowed by permit in the Little River Management Area). Horseback riding and climbing are also permitted.

After seeing the beauty of Little River in Cherokee County, one will quickly find that the wondrous and awe-inspiring views do not end there. The Little River empties into Weiss Lake, The Crappie Fishing Capital of the World. The lake consists of 30,200 acres of beauty and natural wonder, for avid fishermen and water lovers alike.

Though it's known as the crappie capital, largemouth and striped bass are also frequent biters, and some are over 25 pounds. The beauty of Weiss Lake is stunning from every angle. Atop Cherokee Rock Village, one can see the lake and the natural beauty that surrounds it. From a lakeside pier, one can view the almost 450 miles of shoreline and the vast blue waters meeting the skyline. The sides of the lake are lined with beautiful, resort style retreats. The area is known for its unsurpassed beauty and love for fisherman, and neither a bait shop nor a natural wonder will be difficult to find.

Cherokee Rock Village

If you'd like to view Weiss Lake as the local bald eagles do, Cherokee Rock Village (also known as Little Rock City) provides the perfect spot. Astounding views are seen from the parking lot and become increasingly breathtaking as one explores the park. Though locally famous for its bolted rock climbing routes, easy strolls can still lead right to a bird's eye view of Weiss Lake and the two states below. It is not unusual to be able to look down on soaring birds of prey, and bird watchers will likely find this to be one of the best spots in the state for birding.

Some of the rock formations are up to 300 million years old, and Cherokee natives used the area for ceremonies before the Trail of Tears. Years later, during the Civil War, it was used by both Northern and Southern troops. The area consists of 200 acres that sprawl above and along the side of Lookout Mountain and has several trails, caves, climbing routes, and bouldering and repelling sites. The Southeastern Climbers Coalition sponsors a competition on site attracting more than 100 climbers annually, and the rocks are often referred to as being "larger than houses" or "mansion-sized."

The history surrounding it provides the perfect spot for primitive camping on the rocks, with ghost stories told over campfires. A sunrise seen here provides an almost spiritual experience, as the mist hovers over Weiss Lake, and one envisions old times of a Native American's morning. They lived among the very caves in which children explore today. They awoke atop the mountain to see the sunrise top the gigantic rocks and looked down on eagles soaring above a steaming Weiss Lake. The land was sacred, just like the many memories made here over the thousands of years. A best kept secret of Alabama, Cherokee Rock Village is an absolute must-see for those visiting the northern area of the state.

Horse Pens 40

South of Cherokee Rock Village is Horse Pens 40, most commonly known for its bouldering. Home to some of the oldest naturally exposed stones on the planet, Horse Pens 40 also has a place in Native American History.

The boulders sit atop Chandler Mountain and contain Native American burial grounds. Over the course of the 15,000 years of human habitation that has existed at the park, it has been home to both Cherokee and Creek Indians. It was once used for strategic purposes during war, the boulders acting as fortresses. They used the landscape to trap horses, and during peace time, the area was used for both shelter and ceremonial purposes. In fact, there is only one peace treaty ever signed between the Creek and Cherokee Indians, and it was signed at Horse Pens 40.

During the Civil War, confederate soldiers and southern residents realized the strategic advantages of the area and hid personal belongings and troop supplies here to guard them from the Union.

In modern times, the boulders are used for sport, but also for acoustics, as the park serves as a natural amphitheater for art and music festivals. It is known by the state as the Home of the South's Bluegrass Music and is known as one of the top bouldering fields in the United States. There is a strict no pet policy here, due to the rare and endangered rock species in the park, but camp sites are available.

Lake Guntersville State Park

If you're looking for a "one size fits all" vacation spot in Alabama, Lake Guntersville State Park should be one of your first stops. It's quite tucked away, and cellphone service is limited in some areas. Though very much worth the trip, you'll want to be sure you have a map or printed directions to your destination; there's a significant chance your GPS will lose service once you are about half an hour away from the park.

Once inside the park, you'll see an astonishing 18-hole championship golf course. There's also a beach – complete with sand – on the lake. Tucked away among 6,000 acres of woodlands, the Lake Guntersville State Park Lodge lies between the luscious rolling hills of the golf course and a majestic 69,000 acre lake. From the lodge, one can step out onto one of multiple balconies for a view that would leave anyone breathless.

The Lodge has rooms with an assortment of beautiful views, and cottages on the lake may be rented through the lodge and local independents. It's worth noting that, aside from the lodge, local dining options are limited, and you may find yourself driving up to half an hour, depending on your lodging area. However, most cottages in the area have full kitchens and grills, and the Lodge has a restaurant that serves three meals daily.

The Walls of Jericho

The Walls of Jericho, another spectacular Alabama wonder, are located primarily in Jackson County, which has the highest number of caves of any county in the United States. The Walls are often referred to as "The Grand Canyon of the South." Davy Crockett's family owned land here, and he explored the area in the late 1700's. Though the property extends into Tennessee, most of its acreage is in Alabama.

The Walls of Jericho contain several rare species of wildlife. The Pale Lilliput and Alabama Lampshell Muscles do not exist in any other area of the world. The Paint River, the body of water that beautifully graces the Walls, is home to a number of federally and globally endangered fish. Overall, there are close to 100 species of fish in Paint Rock River.

The Walls are a bit of a hidden wonder, in part due to the arduous hiking involved to get the best of views. The hike is over two miles on a hill (downhill upon entering, all uphill and quite taxing upon exiting). Hikers should plan for a full six hours if they plan to enjoy the gorge and as much of its beauty as possible. Given the hazards of the trail (several streams must be crossed in order to get to the gorge, and the streams can rise quickly during heavy rains), it is highly suggested that visitors plan ahead by wearing comfortable clothing and shoes and packing plenty of snacks and water.

If the trail is too strenuous to walk, a horse ride is also

available for those still wishing to explore. This trail is over eight miles long but still leads down into the gorge. Once inside the gorge, you're sure to be left breathless at the 150 foot wide limestone canyon, as you look up to the 200 foot tall cliffs above.

Despite having only been open to the public since 2004, and contrary to its lack of publicity, it's estimated that up to 300 people visit the Walls each weekend during peak season. Camp sites are also available, but only primitive sites are offered, as no electricity or facilities are provided.

Ghost Towns

Some of Alabama's ghost towns are just that – simply empty towns haunted by the ruins of buildings that once stood over disappearing populations. Others have been transformed into State Parks, preserving their artifacts and working with locals to piece together their histories. Ghost towns certainly aren't a part of the South you'd expect to see. After all, most of them were created out west after people gradually settled into more fertile lands or moved after the gold rush had exhausted its fame.

However, Alabama didn't exactly have an easy road in the beginning of its statehood. Early settlements took place among the many rivers, lakes, and bays, before flooding risks were understood. This led to major flooding, spreading of malaria, and abandonment of the towns.

Recent trends show that the state is working to preserve what's left of some of these ghost towns, so that this significant part of Alabama history may be treasured and not forgotten. When visiting some of these sites, one should keep in mind that some of the preservations are only possible with donations received. Therefore, each visitor is asked to take care to do his or her part by leaving the ruins just as they are found, as well as considering making a small donation to their up-keep.

Blakeley

In Baldwin County, all that remains of the ghost town, Blakeley, is a cemetery containing mass graves for fever victims, jail ruins, and an overgrown forest full of massive oak trees. During the Creek War (1813-1814), most nearby towns, including Fort Mims, were destroyed. Blakely became the county's first seat after being spared and began to thrive as a river port, rivaling Mobile.

However, the very waters that led to the shipping port also fed the swamps of the Mobile-Tensaw Delta. Soon, a mysterious epidemic began to spread, killing several residents and driving others out of the town in fear. Residents blamed the bad, swampy air for the sudden illnesses. However, the waters, full of mosquitoes, led to massive outbreaks of malaria and yellow fever. The epidemic's true cause was discovered long after the town had been deserted.

Today, the old town of Blakeley is a State Park, and the ruins of the town may be explored, along with vague outlines of the old streets. According to legend, one of the massive oak trees was the town's official hanging tree for criminals sentenced to death and still remains somewhere on the grounds.

Fort Mims

Fort Mims was built in 1813. It once held over 100 houses and about 500 residents, all surrounded by a fort.

However, the Creek Indians invaded the town, and it was burned to the ground in its entirety. The fort and houses were destroyed, and its residents massacred, leaving only 36 survivors.

Chilton County

Chilton County's first gold discovery was near the Coosa River. Most of the gold was found near the Piedmont Upland, in the counties surrounding Coosa County. Two decades later, Alabama's gold treasures were soon forgotten and left behind for the California Gold Rush.

Maplesville

Maplesville was once located about three miles from its present location, on Highway 191. However, nothing remains of the old town except the cemetery.

Stanton

Six miles south of current Maplesville lies another ghost town, Stanton. Union troops fired on the Confederates from behind the town's post office, and many civil war artifacts have been found near the church that still remains. The church, post office, and a few houses are all that remain of this historical town.

Tannehill State Park

Tannehill State Park, though now a major tourist destination, was once a town thriving on its iron production. The town was destroyed during the Civil War, and there are several legends about the hidden treasures that have yet to be found in the area.

Amber Richards

Claiborne

Claiborne, about 90 minutes northeast of Mobile, was another thriving port city in the 1800s. The town also had several cotton gins, although present day, one will likely see no more than a few homes, three cemeteries with headstones dated from the 1700s, and the river landing. In its prime, the town held 5,000 residents, though they'd soon be sick with many of the plagues that sunk the towns around them.

Yellow fever and cholera struck the town, and not long afterward, the Union troops began occupying Alabama. By 1865, the war had ended and the town became filled with loiterers looking for valuables. The town then had little left to offer other than its shipping port, which was hanging by a thread, along with the town's population.

By the 1900's, the railroad was built nearby, and cotton shipments were transported by railway instead of steamboat. Now, most of the town that was preserved has been moved to nearby Purdue Hill.

Another well-kept secret of Claiborne is the former home of William B. Travis. Colonel Travis actually left Claiborne to fight in the Texas Revolution and became the Texan Commander at the Battle of the Alamo. Travis was killed during the battle, and his home has since been moved to Purdue Hill, along with other parts of Old Claiborne. Today, one may tour the home and find the furniture staged just as it was when he resided there.

St. Stephens

St. Stephens (now part of Old St. Stephens Historical

Park) was once a prosperous Alabama town, well ahead of its time for a southern town in the 1800s. The town is believed to have featured a theater, opera, and racetrack. Though nothing is left of the town today, archeologists and historians are still putting together the pieces after digging up what is thought to be old brick sidewalks, as well as gold and silver.

It is believed that the town had scores of saloons and an average of only four people to each home. Unusually for its time and area, according to historians, St. Stephens also had several hotels. When Alabama was simply a territory, the town served as its first capital. Over time, the town's 2,000 residents began to slowly decline, at first due to the capital's relocation to Old Cahawba.

However, the town was located on the Tom Bigbee

River, and like most southern river- and bay- side settlements, the residents soon began losing battles with yellow fever. The town became virtually abandoned a short time later, and by the Civil War era, many of the town's buildings had been destroyed for Confederate salt works.

The historical park offers camping, bird watching, and fishing among its 200 acres and has a 100 acre lake. However, not much remains of the old territorial capital, other than replicated street signs and plaques commemorating what once stood.

Old Cahawba

Of the 17 ghost towns in Alabama, the most famous is Old Cahawba, which was the first state capital. Located near Selma, the town became virtually deserted after the Civil War.

49

The abandonment was due to a Union blockade that halted cotton shipments.

In 1863, the Cahawba Military Prison was open, and it immediately held over 600 men. As the war progressed, conditions became horrendous as the population began to exceed 3,000 prisoners. Despite a severe lack of food and supplies, less than 150 men died. However, when the survivors boarded the steamboat for home, tragedy struck again. The steamboat exploded on the Mississippi River, killing 2,000 men.

Today, the remains of Old Cahawba may still be seen at the archeological site. Visitors will find wells still flowing with water, an abandoned capital building, slave quarters, the Cahawba Military Prison, and church ruins. The area features picnic areas and a boat ramp, and three cemeteries still remain.

Autauga County Ghost Towns

Autauga County has three ghost towns, two of which were once county seats. One abandoned county seat is a mere 10 acres, just four miles south of Prattville. Named Washington, after George Washington, it was the first county seat. The county grew more than expected, however, and residents soon began to realize its location was less than ideal. Thus, it was abandoned for a better location, as were many historic government sites.

The second, adjacent to present day Kingston, was the new government center of choice, but it was shortly abandoned as well, leaving behind little more than a cemetery. Another in the county, though not a political site,

was established in 1820 and may be found near present day

Minton. The community was abandoned after the flooding of

Mulberry Creek in 1880.

Beautiful Scenic Drives to Take

Popular among motorcyclists, Highway 25 is said to be comparable to cyclist routes in California, featuring curves and switchbacks. The ride is very smooth, with the pavement well maintained. The route is scenic, significantly wooded, and runs south to north through Bibb, Shelby, Jefferson, and St. Clair counties. The route ends at 29 Dreams Motorcycle Resort.

Talladega Scenic Drive

A beautiful drive, located about 70 miles east of Birmingham, may be found traveling down Highway 281 through Talladega National Forest. Often called the Talladega Scenic Drive, the route is less than 50 miles long, but has

53

astounding views of the Appalachian Mountain foothills. This route is located near Cheaha State park, where travelers can stop and take a detour to see the highest point in Alabama.

Highway 411 – Nature, Lakes, and Locally Famous Barbecue

If you're simply up for a nature ride, Highway 411 will provide some stunning scenery at times, if you travel the highway straight from Ashville's farmland into the Weiss Lake area, where Cherokee Rock Village can be seen on the side of Lookout Mountain. Through a large portion of Etowah County, the highway runs parallel to the beautiful Coosa River. Once the highway runs into Cherokee County, it's only a quick detour to visit Little River Canyon.

It's worth mentioning that along this route, in

Rainbow City, the uncontested favorite barbecue in the area is found at Local Joe's. True to its name, most of the products sold in the market, including the meat, are from local farmers. The market smokes some of the most savory meat in the south for a full 24 hours, creating an unforgettable flavor that keeps locals frequently driving from up to an hour away just for a taste.

Their selection changes seasonally but typically consists of locally farmed meats, such as turkey, pork, and ham. Locals claim the smoked ribs, with Local Joe's special sauce, are the best in the state. The market also has savory baked goods made in-house and sells everything from local honey to local wine.

U.S. Highway 72 – The Trail of Tears

Following U.S. Highway 72 from Ross Landing, Tennessee to Waterloo, Alabama, one can very closely follow the same route as the Cherokee Indians' Trail of Tears. Over one thousand Native Americans were removed from the area and displaced to Oklahoma under a Presidential Mandate.

The Trail of Tears Commemoration and Motorcycle Ride seeks to preserve this knowledge, as well as honor the event annually to raise awareness. Often called the "Drane/Hood Overland Route," it is officially recognized as the Trail of Tears Corridor. Alabama Waterfowl Association sponsors an annual bike ride; in which most of the proceeds go toward raising awareness about the Indian Removal Act.

Signs and historical markers have been placed along the route thanks to previous contributors. The ride began in

1994 and continues to annually honor the lives of the First

Americans that were taken 150 years ago.

Special Attractions and Must-See Places to Visit

Motorsports

As previously mentioned, Talladega boasts one of the toughest tracks in Nascar Racing, and the Magic City is home to the Barber Vintage Motor Sports Museum, with vintage motorcycles dating as early as 1902. On the same property, Barber boasts an 830 acre park with 2.38 miles of track for racing. In addition to races and the museum, there are various events held here throughout the year, and even Porsche chose the location for their Sport Driving School. The company stated that this was not only due to the challenging course, but also the reputation the track has built as a friendly environment.

Troy University Rosa Parks Museum in Montgomery

The legacy of Civil Rights Activist, Rosa Parks, may be seen at the Troy University Rosa Park Museum in Montgomery. The museum is centered on the events that led to the bus boycott, when Rosa Parks, who was black, sat in a "white section only" area of a local bus. The museum is located at the former site of the theater where Rosa Parks made history, in a bus parked in front of the building.

The original buildings in the area, including the Empire Theater, were considered impossible to restore and were demolished. Troy University bought the property with plans to build a parking deck. However, the University soon began to take note of public interest in the site's history and began plans to honor Rosa Parks with the museum. After an abundance of donations and federal grant money, the museum opened exactly 45 years after Park's historical arrest in 1955.

The museum features six different areas, one of which is primarily for children, which tell the story of Rosa Parks and the other civil rights activists of her time. Visitors may begin by learning about the era in which the boycott took place and learning about the early life of Parks before she took her stand. Visitors then have the opportunity to hear the personal testimonials of those who participated in the boycott.

There's even a "Bus Room," which features a bus from the era. The actual arrest record from 1955 may be seen, as well as a reenactment of the bus boycott. Virtually every aspect of the boycott may be explored here; there's even an area dedicated to the ways in which transportation had to be organized (such as the famous Rolling Church Buses) for those participating in the boycott. The final area is called "The Victory Room" and shows features that highlight the day Martin Luther King, Jr., along with other former protestors, rode in the front seats of buses.

The children's area features the Cleveland City Time Machine, which is a 1950's era bus with special effects. It essentially takes children back in time to the 1800s to see the abundant segregation and the fights of those such as Harriet Tubman and Dred Scott.

The museum, a nonprofit organization, has an informational kiosk that lists other sites in Alabama that were considered central to the Civil Rights Movement. Annual events are hosted to honor both the anniversary of Park's arrest (in December) and her birthday (in February).

The Troy University Rosa Parks Museum and Library are located in the same building. The museum is located on the first floor. The second floor hosts a research center, with a multitude of resources about the Bus Boycott and its legal challenges.

Cheaha Mountain

This mountain is great for those loving the outdoors. It is the highest point in Alabama, and has a lookout tower at the top called Bunker Tower. At the base of the mountain are many restaurants, cottages and chalets to stay in, swimming pools and hotels. Popular for hiking and climbing activites.

Confederate White House

For less than a year, Montgomery was considered the capital of the Confederacy, until it was relocated to

Richmond, Virginia. The only Confederate President, Jefferson Davis, and his family resided at the White House in Alabama until the capital was moved. Having served as the first capital of the Confederacy, it is now open to the public and features original furnishings from the era. Personal items of the Davis family are also on display.

The home was built in the 1830's by an ancestor of F. Scott Fitzgerald's wife. The home spent its next 30 years among several owners, but was remodeled before its use as the White House between February and May of 1861. It is said that Mrs. Davis had exquisite taste, as she hired a French chef for the home before the official move, and frequently wore French gowns while traveling in an elaborate carriage.

Amazingly, the home was obtained as the White House

for $5,000 per year from its previous owner. The Italianate style home quickly became the social center of the South, in part due to Mrs. Davis' elegant taste and hospitality. Numerous writers often wrote of her charm, as well as that of the home.

The First White House of the Confederacy is located across from the current Alabama State Capitol, in the downtown area of historic Montgomery.

Trail of Tears Riverwalk – Waterloo

A paved riverwalk, as well as a retaining wall to prevent erosion, have both been built using bricks purchased to support the cause. A memorial statue is also being built with proceeds, all in honor of the displaced and fallen Native Americans who were victims of the Indian Removal Act.

Alabama was a major focal point during the Trail of Tears, after the passage of the Indian Removal Act in 1830. President Jackson signed the bill into law as a Presidential Mandate, despite the bill's lack of public support. The Cherokees, challenged the Act through the Supreme Court, claiming to be an independent nation.

Their claims were successful, and Chief Justice John Marshall claimed the acts were invalid, because the sovereign Nation of the Cherokees would have to sign a treaty and have it ratified in order to be removed. An estimated 96% of Cherokees stood by the decision of Justice Marshall. However, a tiny minority followed Cherokee leader Major Ridge.

Convinced the fight was hopeless, Ridge agreed to sell

Cherokee lands in exchange for money and land in

Oklahoma. A backdoor treaty (The Treaty of New Echota)

was signed among the few, and suddenly Jackson had the

legal power he needed to remove the Cherokees. Though the

Cherokees continued to fight the betrayal, they were

unsuccessful. Within two years of the treaty's signing, the

forced removal began.

Martin Van Buren, just one year into his term as the

nation's eighth president, commanded U.S. General Winfield

Scott to gather as many Cherokees as possible throughout

Tennessee, Alabama, and Georgia. About 1,200 Cherokees

were placed in a concentration camp in Fort Payne, Alabama.

Another 17,000 were placed in concentration camps

near present day Chattanooga. Five thousand were moved to

Oklahoma by boat, but a timely drought lowered the rivers too much to send any others. Conditions in the camps were becoming very deadly quickly, as illnesses began to spread.

The government decided to relocate over a thousand Cherokees they considered "rebellious" to Waterloo, thus beginning the Trail of Tears through northern Alabama. Major Ridge was labeled as a coward and traitor and was executed in 1839.

Fort Payne Cabin Site

A majority of the Cherokees forced out by troops were driven out of Fort Payne. Federal troops established forts for the purposes of forced removal, and the Fort Payne Cabin Site (located near Fourth Street SE and Gault Avenue S) was one of over 20 locations seized by the military for this purpose. The cabin is thought to have belonged to a Cherokee and was built around 1825. Today, it is merely an empty cabin foundation and chimney. The site is open to the public but must be toured by appointment only. 256-845-6888 can be called to schedule a visit.

Robert Trent Jones Golf Trail

Although the state is known for its beautiful, abundant waters, it is, after all, Alabama the Beautiful. Among this beauty lies the largest attempt at golf course construction ever made: The world famous Robert Trent Jones Golf Trail. The trail stretches from Muscle Shoals to Mobile, so no matter where you are in the state, you are bound to be near one of its 468 holes.

Some of the holes, by the way, are simply

breathtaking. From 80 foot waterfalls to cliffs overlooking the Tennessee River, you'll find that even our golf trails embrace the beauty of our waters.

Mobile - Azalea Trail Maids

If you're fortunate enough to visit Mobile, you're quite likely to meet a Southern Belle. Mobile very carefully chooses its ambassadors, called Azalea Trail Maids. Often referred to as Southern Belles, you're bound to see them at some historical sites or events around the city. They've been in Macy's parades and were also invited by the Presidential Inaugural Committee to represent the state during President Obama's inauguration.

The Trail Maids represent Mobile and its three centuries of history and have been ambassadors for the past six decades. The tradition began in 1929, when Mobile hosted

the Azalea Trail Marathon. City residents were encouraged to

plant azaleas along their streets, creating an azalea trail, and

the maids came out in antebellum ball gowns, sharing

historical information with guests. Later, the group grew to 50

and current-day Maids must meet exceptional qualifications

in order to become an ambassador for their city.

Not only do the potential Maids have to be Mobile

residents, but they also must be high school juniors with 3.0

or higher GPAs and be active in their community. They are

then interviewed by a panel of judges and chosen by their

school's sponsor, and the final group goes to a city interview

with another judge panel. The decisions are then based on

overall school performance, poise, and knowledge of the city,

among other qualities. To this day, the maids wear Old South style ball gowns and are meant to represent the history of a true southern belle in Old Mobile.

USS Alabama battleship

The USS Alabama battleship is half as long as the Empire State Building is tall and was towed more than 1,000 miles to its home on Mobile Bay. During the Battle of the Philippine Sea, the ship shot down nine enemy planes. It fired 1,500 tons of shells into military and factory sites near Tokyo. It now serves as a museum site, next to the submarine, USS Drum. The submarine also endured heavy combat during World War II and remained intact during Hurricane Katrina. Both vessels are open daily for fascinating, historical, self-guided tours.

Dauphin Island

Dauphin Island is three miles off the coast of Mobile, and the entire island is designated as a bird sanctuary. Tourists flock to see the massive bird migrations on the island. The

State of Alabama's Marine Science Institution is located on the island as well, and it is home to Dauphin Island Sea Lab. The Sea Lab's grounds were once owned by the Air Force, but are now home to an aquarium specifically designed to specialize in estuarine organisms. There is a Marsh Boardwalk and a hall that features exhibits focusing on local aquatic life.

"Iron Bowl" Traditions

If you're blessed enough to be in Alabama during football season, as a sports fan, it's an absolute must to go to an Alabama or Auburn football game. The rivalry, as mentioned previously, is one of the most intense in the nation among college football. Your jaw may drop as you begin to hear southern belles "trash talking" even their closest family members. At first glance, it's certain to appear hostile, until you see that fans are thick skinned and passionate. At the end

of the day, you may even see them as fun loving! It's true –

fans have football personalities that are compartmentalized,

and it's not unusual at all for a trash talking southern belle to

pick back up the southern hospitality and grace just after the

game clock stops.

While visiting an Auburn home game, you'll see

crowds gathering at Toomer's Corner to celebrate. It's an old

tradition that stems from rolling the 80 year old oak trees that

once stood at the corner, until they died prematurely a few

seasons ago. Toomer's Drugs, on the corner where the

celebrations are held, has locally famous, fresh-squeezed

lemonade. An abundance of souvenir shops are also located

in the neighborhood.

If visiting an Alabama home game, you'll likely want to visit the Paul W. Bryant Museum, locally called the "Bear Bryant Museum," based on the coach's nickname. In 1981, Bryant suggested opening a museum that honored former players and coaches of the sport. Today, it centers on the rich history of Alabama football, including Paul "Bear" Bryant and his legendary coaching career. The museum features artifacts and memorabilia, commemorating the University of Alabama's football program.

Monroeville: "The Literary Capital of Alabama"

Monroeville, considered the literary capital of Alabama, was home to Nelle Harper Lee. Lee was the author of the Pulitzer Prize winning book, *To Kill a Mockingbird*, and won a Presidential Medal of Freedom for the book, which paints a realistic portrait of the racism experienced in

Monroeville's past.

Each year, the town hosts the Alabama Writers Symposium at Alabama Southern Community College, for an annual weekend of lectures and literary discussions, and awards a "Harper Lee Award for Alabama's Distinguished Writer of the Year."

The town also hosts a theatrical performance of *To Kill a Mockingbird* each spring, as it has for over 20 years. The performance is interactive, selecting audience members as jurors. The event's tickets sell very quickly, so it's important to plan ahead if this is an experience you're hoping to enjoy while in Alabama.

While touring this literary beauty of the town, you'll

notice the famous clock tower on the top of the historic courthouse. The Courthouse Museum is open for tours, and inside, visitors will discover photos, exhibits, personal stories about Nelle Harper Lee, and the courthouse that inspired the set for the movie. Harper's father, an attorney, often practiced law in the very same courtroom.

The novel and movie are based on a fictional town called Maycomb, Alabama, and a young black man who was placed on trial for attacking a white woman during one of the South's most racist eras. Locals claim one of the book's characters, Dill, who was a childhood friend of the main character's, is based on Truman Capote. Capote was a neighbor and childhood friend of Harper's, and wrote *In Cold Blood*, as well as *Breakfast at Tiffany's*.

Monroeville was also once home to Truman Capote,

Mark Childress, and other famous writers.

Amusement Parks to Visit

Adventure Land

Adventure Land, located in Dothan, offers kid friendly attractions, as well as some fun for the adults. The park has a jungle miniature golf course with 18 holes, and another similar waterfall course. Bumper boats, batting cages, and go-kart tracks are sure to win over children of all ages, and no amusement park would be complete without an arcade.

Splash Adventure

Formerly Alabama Adventure, Splash Adventure is now exclusively a water park, offering everything from thrill rides to lazy rivers. On a hot summer day in Alabama, children of all ages will be thrilled to arrive at this Birmingham area attraction, located in Bessemer. Areas of the park are geared toward its younger visitors, with interactive play and water activity areas. Families are sure to enjoy the half-pipe water slides and the unique "Splashdown," which sends riders into a giant swirl and tosses them into a splash pool.

Waterville

Perfect for beach goers or anyone headed south during an Alabama summer, Waterville offers 12 assorted water attractions. The lazy river, called "Crystal Waters River," can guide passengers underneath the waterfall for a quick cool off. Rainbow Falls, however, is sure to provide a rush and a splash, as riders spiral down assorted half-pipe slides. The "Screamin' Demon" is seemingly vertical at first, with 60 feet of acceleration before sliding into a splash pool.

Southern Adventure

Located in Huntsville, Southern Adventures offers miniature golf, bumper cars, a rock climbing wall, and water attractions. Batting cages may also be enjoyed, along with go-carts and carnival rides. This park is open year round.

A Local's Favorite Places

My favorite part of the state is the Northeastern area. Here, the Coosa River is located where an abundance of festivals are held throughout the summer. The scenic route, along the Coosa, eventually leads to the areas of Weiss Lake and Cherokee Rock Village, which are a short drive from Little River Canyon. There's also the "Secret Bed and Breakfast," overlooking Weiss Lake with a rooftop pool, walking trails, and even cabins.

This area is ideal for primitive camping, particularly Cherokee Rock Village, because the giant rock formations provide excellent shade on hot days. The Cherokee County area offers kayaking, fishing, superb camping locations, and serene views. Though you won't find many hotels in the area, if you're looking for less primitive accommodations, there are resort-style condos and homes for rent along the side of Weiss Lake. The Northeastern area of Alabama is a boater's haven, as there are multitudes of boat ramps for the beautiful lakes, rivers, and creeks.

Tied for favorite, however, is the Alabama Gulf Coast. Yes, the sand really is as white as sugar; yes, the FloraBama is all that it is cracked up to be. It's the picture-perfect place

to experience southern hospitality and the beach life. The

sand here is appreciated so much so that it is even exported to

areas of the Mississippi coast. Visitors can deep-sea fish to

catch their own dinner, or rent watercrafts of all sizes for a

day on the water.

I personally enjoy the Moss Rock Preserve area, near

Birmingham. Located in Hoover, Moss Rock hosts a number

of festivals each year. In the fall, an art and eco fest, called

simply "Moss Rock Festival," offers shuttle services and

charges no admission for a festival sure to thrill the entire

family. Artists, bakeries, food trucks, live music, and eco-

friendly designs and products are just a hint of the activities

offered at this festival, which occurs in the fall after the

Alabama sun has had a chance to cool. Year round, however,

one can explore the trails at Moss Rock to find beautiful creeks, boulders, and plaques detailing different plant species that can be seen on the hike.

The Cullman area also is quite fascinating, as it is the former home of country icon, Hank Williams, Jr. Williams was recently the headliner of "Rock the South," a musical festival new to the Cullman area that has a unique purpose. The area was victim to the April 27, 2011 tornado outbreak, which was catastrophic. "Rock the South" is said to represent when the tornado rocked the area, and the extraordinary recovery that immediately followed. In Alabama, already known for our hospitality, but when disaster strikes, it shines astoundingly. The community spirit in the state suddenly takes over the college rivalries, and our close-knit communities bond together like nothing found "in the North," as locals say. "Rock the South" is a perfect representation of the many times our communities have fought together to recover from tornado outbreaks, ice storms, and floods.

Cullman is also home to Ava Maria Grotto, which is a four acre religious park, with 125 miniature reproductions of religiously significant buildings throughout the world. The reproductions were created by a Benedictine Monk in the late 1800s and were completed in the 1950s. A majority of the materials used for the reproductions were donated, and the details of the sculptures are astoundingly realistic. The park is located at Alabama's first Benedictine Abby, which is still the only one in the state. In the gift shops, visitors will find goods, such as candles and sculptures, made on site.

Annual Festivals and Fairs

Taking in various fairs and festivals are a great pastime too, both for romantic dates for something different, a family outing, or just an excuse for a drive and destination to visit. Below you'll find a partial list of festivals to visit in Alabama. Each festival is hyperlinked to take you to the page of the festival's site for more specifics.

February

Mardis Gras, Mobile

http://www.mobilemardigras.com/main.html

Hosting the oldest Mardi Gras carnival in the nation, Mobile celebrates a variety of cultures and religions as part of this festival. The celebration is virtually unlimited and often hosts parades, huge crowds, trinket tosses.

Downtown Gadsden Chili Cookoff, Gadsden

http://www.downtowngadsden.com/

Warm up with a bowl of chili and vote for the crowd favorite, or cook up a batch of your own to be eligible for prizes.

March

Anniversary of Battle of Horseshoe Bend, Dadeville

http://www.topeventsusa.com/alabama-battle-of-horseshoe-bend.html

This anniversary celebration recreates life in the era of the 1800's. It depicts Cherokee and Creek Indians and life of those on the frontier. It takes place on the site of the original battle.

Alabama Chocolate Festival, Rainbow City

http://www.rbcalabama.com/html/chocolate_festival.html

Live entertainment is the backdrop for all things chocolate at this one of a kind festival. Give aways, scavenger hunts, egg tosses and children activities are just some of the ways visitors can have their chocolate and eat it, too!

April

Anniversary of the Battle of Selma, Selma

http://www.battleofselma.com/

This anniversary celebration is a re-enactment of the Battle of Selma, including cannon blasts between the Union and Confederate soldiers during two battles. There is also a grand ball, a ladies tea and even a camp dance.

Toadlick Music Festival, Dothan

http://www.toadlick.com/

This Country, Rock and Southern Rock music festival is a three day extravaganza that's great for the soul. The most recent festival led to a donation of over $4,000 to a local food bank. Previous acts include The Band Perry, Trace Atkins, Dierks Bentley.

Alabama Book Festival, Montgomery

http://www.alabamabookfestival.org/

The festival provides free workshops and children activities, including scavenger hunts and giant crossword puzzles.

May

Alabama Jubilee Hot Air Balloon Classic, Decatur

http://alabamajubilee.net/

This free event is full of celebrations to delight all ages. Over 60 hot air balloons are part of the festival, glowing at night, at flight during the day and providing balloon rides around sunset. There are also fireworks and tractor attractions.

Limestone Sheriff's Rodeo, Athens

http://www.limestonesheriffrodeo.com/

Each year, the limestone sheriff's department hosts the rodeo the third weekend in May. The event provides funding for the law enforcement and features classic rodeo competitions, street dance, a parade and more.

Annual Down Home Blues Festival, Huntsville

http://www.zvents.com/huntsville_al/events/show/262021065

-down-home-blues-festival

Celebrate new and classic music with soul and blues

artists.

June

The Miracle Worker Play, Tuscumbia (occurs each weekend in June and July)

http://www.helenkellerbirthplace.org/

This annual celebration honors the achievements of deaf and blind, Helen Keller, and her "miracle worker," Anne Sullivan. The show is presented in a Broadway style and takes place annually at the birthplace of Keller.

Alabama Blueberry Festival, Brewton

http://www.alabamablueberryfestival.com/

This festival features a food court and live entertainment. Of course, visitors may also buy fresh blueberries, blueberry bushes, blueberry ice cream and cookbooks.

Gadsden Riverfest, Gadsden

http://www.gadsdenriverfest.com/

Tens of thousands of people enjoy this festival each year. Enjoy high profile musical guests, local vendors and children activities, all alongside the beautiful Coosa River. Previous acts include Randy Travis, Keith Urban, Daughtry and the Commodores.

July

Spirit of America Festival, Decatur

http://www.spiritofamericafestival.com/

A free event at Point Mallard Park, this celebration features live music, a local pageant and fireworks show.

WC Handy Music Festival, Florence

http://www.wchandymusicfestival.org/

This an all week celebration throughout the city

honoring the area's musical history with parades, concerts and blues legends. In the past, the festival has hosted acts such as Charlie Byrd and Ramsey Lewis.

Alabama Deep Sea Fishing Rodeo, Dauphin Island
http://www.adsfr.com/

Anglers from several states compete in a deep sea fishing tournament in the Gulf for a chance to win almost half a million dollars in prizes, including cash.

Thunder on the Mountain, Birmingham
http://www.thunderonthemountainbirmingham.com/

The state's largest fireworks display sparkles above Vulcan and may be seen from miles away.

August

Alabama Restaurant Week, Statewide

http://www.ilovealabamafood.com/alabama-food/art-of-alabama-food-exhibit-tours-the-state-hitting-birmingham-orange-beach-and-beyond/

Over 200 restaurants participate. Special menus and pricing are offered throughout the week. Some of the dishes featured may be seen in the brochure "100 Dishes to Eat in Alabama Before You Die." In Alabama, our soul food is a serious topic.

World's Longest Yard Sale, Gadsden

http://www.lookoutmountainparkway.org/yardsale.html

This record breaking 690 mile yard sale begins in Gadsden and heads north.

Black Belt Folk Roots Festival, Eutaw

http://eutawchamber.com/events.htm

Held the fourth weekend in August, this event is organized by the Society of Folk Arts & Culture. Musicians, artists, story tellers and others are brought together at the Greene County Courthouse square each year.

Fort Mims Massacre (Start of Creek War), Tensaw

http://www.fortmims.org/

This anniversary honors the Creek Indian attack on Fort Mims in 1813. The attack killed over 500 settlers. Replicas of militia, settlers and weapons are featured among interactive activities such as Indian crafts.

September

Riverfest Barbecue Cook-off, Decatur

http://www.decaturjaycees.com/riverfest-2012

Barbecue teams from across the South compete for up to $20,000 in prizes. Live music, soul food and children activities provide entertainment for all ages.

Taste of the Bayou, Bayou La Batre

http://alabama.travel/upcoming-events/taste-of-the-bayou-26th-annual

Though tickets are limited to this event, visitors will have access to over 30 booths offering seafood tastings of some of the freshest professionally prepared seafood in the state.

Whistle Stop Festival, Irondale

http://irondalewhistlestopfestival.com/

Known for its legendary fried green tomatoes, the Whistle Stop Café stays open from 9 to 5 during the festival for visitors who come to enjoy the vintage cars and fire engines, food vendors and musicians.

October

Bluff Park Art Show, Hoover

http://www.bluffparkartshow.com/

This is held the first Saturday in October and is a nationally acclaimed art show attracting artists from around the nation for over 50 years.

Magic City Classic, Birmingham

http://www.themagiccityclassic.com/

Famed football rivals, Alabama A&M University and Alabama State University, play annually at Legion Field, the former site of the Iron Bowl.

Bayfest Music Festival, Mobile http://www.bayfest.com/

Multiple stages provide music from almost all genres.

As Alabama's largest music festival, it features over 125 performers. The nonprofit organization provides thousands in scholarships, so visitors can contribute to a great cause while enjoying acts such as B.B. King, Hank Williams, Jr., Journey, Lady Antebellum, Motley Crue and R. Kelly, who have all been performers at the festival.

National Shrimp Festival, Gulf Shores

http://www.myshrimpfest.com/

This festival attracts over 250,000 people after almost half a century of celebration. It features marathons, arts and crafts, entertainment on two stages and of course, shrimp. The sand sculpture competition is sure to thrill this time of year, as the Alabama heat has begun to hide away beneath beautiful, breezy autumn weather.

Cullman October Fest, Cullman

http://www.cullmanoktoberfest.com/

This festival features German traditions such as costumes, food and music. There's also a dog show, kid's area and more. This event is free.

Barber Vintage Festival, Birmingham

http://www.barbervintagefestival.org/

Packed with daredevil action and vintage motorcycles (even the famed Vintage Indian), this festival packs quite a punch. Stunts are performed on vertical walls and through challenging obstacle courses. There is also an antique fire truck exhibit sure to delight all ages.

Colonial Island Dauphine, Dauphin Island

http://www.foodiefestmobile.com/di/history/

This celebration features reenactments with canons on the site of the Battle of Mobile Bay. It's worth noting this site is one of the most endangered historic sites in the nation, and boasts amazing views of the Gulf.

Moundville Native American Festival, Moundville

http://moundville.ua.edu/festival/

This festival celebrates the history and culture of the area's Native Indian tribes. Performers and artists provide entertainment and the area's descendants return to celebrate their heritage each year. The vent is located at the University of Alabama's Moundville Archaeological Park Wednesday through Saturday during the first full week of October. The festival has native entertainment and interactive activities for most ages.

November

Frank Brown Song writer's Festival http://www.fbisf.com/

This festival has provided a promoting atmosphere for

accomplished and aspiring song writers alike for almost 30 years.

National Veterans Day Parade, Birmingham

http://www.nationalveteransday.org/

Most may not know that the first Veteran's Day celebration in the nation was held in Birmingham, Alabama. The parade draws thousands of participants each year.

Canyon Fest, Fort Payne

http://www.jsu.edu/epic/canyoncenter/

This annual festival is a celebration of nature. Food, vendors, activities and live music are sure to be fun for all ages.

Moss Rock Festival, Hoover

http://www.mossrockfestival.com/

Admission is free to this eco festival featuring virtually everything inspired by nature. Art, food trucks, children's activities, live music and unique nature friendly products are abundant here. Even pets are allowed!

December

Galaxy of Lights, Huntsville (begins in November)

http://www.hsvbg.org/

Held at the Huntsville Botanical Gardens, this holiday light show has over 500 pieces on display and several miles of lights.

Christmas on the River, Demopolis

http://www.demopolischamber.com/COTR/default.asp

Travel along the Tombigbee River to see parades,

fireworks and historic home tours.

Christmas at Eddie's (begins in November)

http://alabama.travel/upcoming-events/christmas-at-eddie-s-26th-annual

This annual tree festival features over 75 themed trees ranging from sports to Victorian style.

Christmas on the Coosa, Wetumpka

http://www.cityofwetumpka.com/Default.asp?ID=361

This festival takes place along the Coosa River and features classic cars, a quilt show and other activities. The festival features a Christmas parade and ends with a fireworks show.

Dangers & Safety Precautions for Alabama

If you plan on spending time in Alabama, chances are that you will be outdoors enjoying our beautiful scenery, music, or shorelines. Though dangers are present in any state while outdoors, the following are threats that are specific to Alabama, among other states. It may be highly unlikely that you encounter any of these, but being prepared is your best defense.

Children's Hospital of Alabama offers a mobile application to identify toxic, poisonous, or venomous dangers in the state. This application is free through iTunes and is called "PoisonPerils." It is important to remember that, should you have an emergency involving contact with any plants, snakes, or insects, to call 911. The poison control hotline may be reached at 1-800-222-1222 for first aid advice while waiting on help to arrive.

General Camping Dangers

Remember that children can overheat more quickly than adults, as their sweat glands are not fully developed enough to cool them.

Remember to teach your children (or anyone else unfamiliar with camping) remember landmarks in case they need to find their way back to camp. This often means looking behind you every so often, so you recognize landmarks from both directions.

Remind members of your group to stay where they are and not panic should they become lost. Children should have a whistle with them, in case of an emergency.

The Alabama sun can cause sunburn very quickly, particularly near our waters. Be sure to wear sunscreen and cotton clothes.

Alabama's weather can change quickly. This means that it is very important to be prepared for storms or a sudden change in temperature, any time you will not have access to indoor shelter.

Precipitation and rapid cooling can be caused by high elevations or windy conditions.

Our summer days can be quite hot, so it's important to structure your activities during the cooler parts of the day, in order to get the most enjoyment of your time, and stay properly hydrated with water.

Be sure to wear hiking shoes (not flip flops, even if it seems cooler) when hiking, and tuck in your pant cuffs to prevent insect bites and other dangers you may not see. Hats can also serve a similar purpose, preventing ticks and other insects from getting into hair.

ALWAYS check the area before setting up camp. Be sure there are no sharp objects (such as broken glass) that could penetrate the tent, causing an unsafe campsite. Also, check for signs of animals, and be sure to avoid campsites prone to "visitors," such as bears. A good rule of thumb is to be sure there isn't any food growing nearby, such as berries, which could attract wildlife.

Before building a firepit, be sure there aren't any local ordinances regarding a dry season (during dry seasons, portable stoves may have to suffice in place of a fire.). Most importantly, be sure the area above your fire is clear of limbs or any other hazard that could catch fire. Fires can spread very quickly in the woods, so it's very important to be proactive.

Packing iodine tablets is a good way to be sure you have emergency access to water IF your supply runs out and you have no other options. Boiling water is another option, to help cleanse water.

Plan to bring enough food for your entire trip and an extra day. It's important to bring foods that may be carried on a hike, such as crackers, trail mix, granola bars, etc.

Do not eat any food found in the wild, such as berries, as poisonous species can be easily mistaken for edible ones.

DEET bug repellants should only be used on children over two years of age, and then only in concentrations less than 30%. Citronella products can also prevent insect bites and should be applied to clothing.

At the end of day, check yourself and your children for ticks. These insects can carry Lyme disease, so it's important to catch them as soon as possible. They often hide in hair, behind the ears, under the arms, and in other hidden areas of the body. Lyme disease typically leaves a red ring around the site of the bite, which can grow up to two inches. Should this appear, seek medical attention.

Before your trip, inform a close friend or family member of your planned destination and when you plan to return home.

Dangerous Plants

1. Poison Ivy – With three leaflets, the edges of the leaves are smooth. It is usually found as a vine, but can also be flat on the ground or growing among bushes. In the spring, this plant can appear with a red color that gradually changes to green. The plant is actively poisonous year round.

2. Poison Oak – This plant also contains three leaflets, with wavy edges. Its top is glossy, with a furry or velvety texture on the underside of the leaves. A times, there will be berries near or attached to the stem. Though it can appear in a vine like pattern, Poison Oak is unable to climb like other vines. This plant follows a typical life cycle, slowly turning to red as autumn approaches. The leaves fall off during the winter.

3. Poison Sumac – This is less common in northern and eastern Alabama, but appears as a bush or small tree. It has 7-13 oval leaflets which may be up to four inches long, and the leaflets often taper to a point. This plant can also produce flowers and berries. Contact with this plant can cause more serious issues than poison oak and poison

ivy (which usually cause a skin rash). Burning poison

sumac in a campfire can be deadly.

Immediately wash the affected area upon contact.

Antihistamines and hydrocortisone cream can help with

allergies and itching symptoms. Be sure that children have

seen pictures of any poisonous plants before entering the

woods, so they know what to avoid.

Dangerous Animals

Wild animals, even small ones, will defend themselves if they feel threatened. Teach children and other unfamiliar campers to never approach a wild animal.

Be sure to keep your camp free of food and odors, and NEVER bring food into tents and sleeping areas. Food should be kept inside your car, or in animal resistant containers if you are far from your vehicle.

For camping, always pack items mentioned above, as well as the following:

Matches (in a waterproof package)

Area maps

Compass (Never rely on a cell phone compass, as lack of

service or unforeseen events can cause it to become inoperable.)

Knife (pocketknife works best)

Extra flashlights

Rain gear (As mentioned previously, storms can approach the area quickly.)

Fire starter

An abundance of clean drinking water

Camping shelter basics (a complete tent with sleeping bags, emergency blanket, first aid kit including tweezers and oral antihistamines, at least 50 feet of nylon rope, a signaling device such as a whistle or pocket flare, and antiseptic soap)

Venomous Snakes

Alabama has six types of snakes with venomous bites.

Though these snakes are dangerous, it is important to remain calm if bitten. Less than one percent of venomous bites from snakes are fatal, and almost half of their bites contain no venom at all. If bitten, it is important to call 911, and then identify the snake. It is acceptable to bring a dead snake (preferably in a sealed container) to the emergency room, but it is CRUCIAL to remember that a dead snake still has reflexes that enable it to bite. NEVER attempt to capture a snake; only take a photo if it is safe to do so.

After calling 911, immediately remove constricting clothing, jewelry, or accessories before the bite begins to swell. If bitten on a limb, be sure to keep the limb above heart level to decrease swelling, but limit movement as much as possible. If safe to do so, wash the affected area. If you choose to arrange your own transport instead of traveling by ambulance, call the emergency facility with as much information as possible, so

the bite can be treated as quickly as possible. NEVER attempt

to cut over the bite, or apply constriction or a cold pack.

Never try to treat the bite yourself, and avoid alcohol and

other medications until a doctor has cleared the victim to do

so.

Copperhead

This snake is found statewide. Its head is yellow to copper red, with lighter colored sides. The color of its tail varies with age, beginning as a yellow and graduating to a dark green or brown in adults. Hourglass patterns are narrower in the center of the back and grow wider along the snake's sides. Though it is venomous, it is the least harmful of the venomous snakes in the state. The average length of a Copperhead is 2 to 3 feet, reaching up to over four feet.

Eastern Coral Snake

Largely found in southern Alabama, this snake is covered in yellow and red rings (the rings touch each other). It has a yellow band across its head and a black ring around its neck. Though they rarely bite unless touched, their venom is compared to that of a Cobra. Its average length is 23 to 32 inches, reaching a maximum of almost four feet.

Eastern Diamondback Rattlesnake

This snake is found in the southern third of Alabama. Its body is olive to brown, often with diamond shapes outlined (usually with a darker outline and a lighter center). Its head is triangular and has diagonal, lightly colored stripes on the side. This snake is considered the most dangerous in the state, with an average length of 3.5-5.5 feet, but it may reach a maximum of up to eight feet.

Water Moccasin (Cotton Mouth)

This snake is found statewide, often near water. It has a triangular head but has less protruding eyes than the harmless snake that closely resembles it. Its body is olive or brown with wide, dark cross bands. The water moccasin also has a dark stripe behind its eye. Its tail is black, and the inside of its mouth is white. These snakes average 30 - 45 inches in length and reach a maximum of around six feet.

Timber or Canebrake Rattlesnake

This snake is found statewide but is more common in

northern and central Alabama. These adult snakes have black

tails with a variety of body colors, ranging from yellow, gray,

or brown. It has black cross bands, edged with white or a pale

shade of yellow. An amber or rust-colored stripe travels down

the middle of its back. Its average length is three to four feet,

reaching a maximum of over six feet.

Pigmy Rattlesnake

This long-tailed snake is found statewide, although it's more

likely to be seen in southern areas of the state. The rattle may not be visible, and its body is often gray, tan, or reddish orange. It has several rows of dark spots or short crossbars. Its average length is between 15 and 22 inches, reaching a maximum of 31 inches.

Poisonous Insects

Because insects are always abundant in outdoor activities, you should become familiar with identifying these. Most of the insects below have a striking resemblance to other, harmless insects. If bitten by an insect you believe to be threatening, call 911. While waiting for help to arrive, the following tips should prove helpful:

1. Remove the stinger with a flat object (such as a library card), but try to   preserve it for optimal treatment.

2. Wash the affected area, and apply a cold compress

for about 10 minutes.

3. If you suspect an allergic reaction, ask the victim if they carry an epinephrine   injection. If so, follow the label, and elevate the victim's legs.

4. If vomiting occurs, be sure the victim turns on his side.

5. If the person is unconscious, administer CPR while waiting on help to arrive.

Poisonous Insects Known to Alabama

Honeybee

Bumblebee

Sweatbee

Fire Ant

Hornet

Saddleback Caterpillar

Scorpion

Wasp/Yellow Jacket

Brown Recluse Spider

Black Widow Spider

Red Velvet Ant/Cow Ant

Dirt Dauber

Special Seasonal Activities

Alabama thrives in the summer. Sure, it may reach 100 degrees, but with a beautiful creek within a few miles of wherever you are in Alabama, combined with our world-famous beaches, you're sure to find a spot to cool off and enjoy some great music and southern hospitality. Our state boasts the beginning of Mardi Gras festivities every spring, and there simply isn't a reason to not visit the Gulf Coast during our spring and summer months.

Mobile and Mardi Gras

Mobile, originally a major shipping port, is known as "The Azalea City," or the New Orleans of Alabama. Although it is a port city, the ship terminals are not used for cruise ships like in other cities. The city is home to Hank Aaron, the first baseball legend to break Babe Ruth's home-run record, which is why it boasts both the Hank Aaron stadium and the Hank Aaron Museum.

Contrary to many beliefs, the first New World Mardi Gras was held in Mobile, not in New Orleans. The carnival season starts in November and stretches through late spring. It is such an instilled part of culture that for local students, the last few days of the season are school holidays.

Even though the heart of downtown was practically a ghost town a few years ago, revitalization has come to Mobile full force via the Mobile Downtown Alliance. The city is full of historic neighborhoods, from colonial to Victorian. In fact, simply strolling through Bienville Park will provide visitors with views of storybook worthy houses and neighborhoods.

Jubilees

If you're into water exploration, Alabama's Delta Resource Center, "Five Rivers," is said to be the best to begin exploring. The Mobile-Tensaw River Delta is one of the nation's largest land-to-ocean transitions, where fresh water from the rivers feed into the salt water from the ocean, creating an estuary system. Because of the many rivers feeding into the Mobile Bay, it is 413 square miles, although its average depth is only 10 feet. However, these shallow waters provide a jubilee for the masses once a year, sometimes more.

Jubilees do not occur in very many areas of the world, but are a phenomenon that brings fish and other seafood into the shallow waters, almost guaranteeing an abundance of seafood catches throughout the event. Though this joyous event has very little scientific study, according to folklore, it typically occurs during the early morning hours of summer months. It occurs when waters are calm and oxygen loss occurs, and the tide brings in ocean water that completely lacks oxygen.

If you're an early riser and happen to visit during a jubilee, you'll likely see massive crowds with nets, baskets and even sacks to catch as much seafood bounty as possible. As the tide approaches, the bounty is pushed and trapped in the shallow beach water, followed by a joyous shout of "Jubilee!" by the large crowds.

Bayfest

The city is, like most in Alabama, famous in part due to its music. Bayfest is Alabama's largest music festival. Hosting over 100 acts and hundreds of thousands of attendees, the festival generates millions for locals and the state. It was recently chosen as a Top 100 event by the American Bus Association, and Top Festival in the Southeast by the Southeastern Tourism Society, among many other honors. It has hosted almost every genre, with artists such as B.B. King, Mary J. Blige, Luke Bryan, and Motley Crue performing over the years.

The Hangout Festival

Nearby, the Hangout Festival occurs in Gulf Shores during the month of May. Although not as large as Bayfest, it hosts fresh seafood vendors, multiple stages, and even a giant water slide on the beach. Visitors may even reserve on-site lockers and rent shuttle services, so the experience is all beach and relaxation, no inconvenience. This festival is a bit newer than Bayfest, but it has still hosted a variety of genres and line ups, including Dave Matthews Band, The Black

Keys, and even Stevie Wonder.

Christmas in Dixie

Bellingrath

Bellingrath Gardens is considered to have the most beautiful Christmas displays in the entire nation (the actual gardens are described in a later section). Bellingrath is illuminated by over 3 million lights. There are nightly choral performances and almost a thousand displays.

Birmingham Zoo

The Magic City of Birmingham also features spectacular lighting events for the season. The Zoolight Safari, hosted by the Birmingham Zoo, not only has synchronized light shows, but also offers train rides and ice skating to boost the holiday spirits of locals and visitors alike.

Gadsden - Winter Wonderland

Though Christmas in Dixie is full of heartwarming hospitality, we rarely see snow around the holidays. However, children will love the interactive snow activities at the Mary G. Hardin Center for Cultural Arts, in Gadsden. The exhibit has an indoor winter wonderland, where kids can toss snowballs, make snow angels, and ride a snow slide.

Huntsville Botanical Gardens

Huntsville hosts one of the South's top lighting events at its Botanical Gardens. Called the Galaxy of Lights, it features over a mile of animated lights, including Santa soaring over a snow covered village. Nursery rhyme characters are also part of this holiday scene, which is sure to delight children and adults of all ages.

Montgomery Zoo

The Montgomery Zoo hosts a very unique lighting event, allowing visitors to take the "Zoofari Skylight" to view the lights from above. There are also traditional pathways to walk, and train rides are available to tour this display with hundreds of thousands of lights.

Gilley's – A Family Tradition

If there's one thing the south has mastered, its tradition. The Gilley family has been a prime example of this, as they carried on their father's on- of-a-kind Christmas tradition for locals to enjoy. In Ballplay, near Hokes Bluff, J.C., Gilley built the county's most marvelous private display of lights in the 1980s, adding a new active light display each year.

Contrary to local legend, Mr. Gilley wasn't an engineer,

though it's easy to see the legend's origin stems from the intricate details of the giant moving structures, some of which were whittled by hand. Mr. Gilley was born into a sawmill family and opened his own mechanic shop, and his combined skills led him to begin a tradition this town simply can't live without.

There's an active manger scene, where Mary churns butter as Joseph taps his foot, along with displays including a cross, an empty tomb, a life sized camel, Santa in an active helicopter, a spinning ferris wheel, and a carousel with wooden horses. Though that would be enough to attract visitors from hours away, there is also an ark with a rainbow shining above, a spinning globe, and two spinning footballs, representing the Iron Bowl rivals.

Mr. Gilley passed away in 2002, and aside from one year when the children's mother was sick, they've carried on the tradition of lighting up the farm each Christmas. Before Mr. Gilley passed, he was always reluctant to put up an optional donation box, but people began donating anyway. It is this box, and the generosity of this close knit community, that keeps this heartwarming annual tradition going in Mr. Gilley's honor.

Public Gardens to Visit

Visiting stunning gardens can be a great way to remember an area. Especially for artists, photographers and avid gardeners. Check out some of these beauties:

Bellingrath Gardens is a 65 acre estate that may be enjoyed on a self-guided walking tour. The estate includes the home and gardens that once belonged to Mr. and Mrs. Bellingrath. The gardens have been public and open year round since 1934. It has been awarded as the top public rose garden in the nation by All-America Rose Selections. Because it lies in the azalea city, of course you will find beautiful azaleas in the spring. However, there is something blooming year round, from roses and chrysanthemums to camellias. In the winter, the gardens also celebrate "Magic

Christmas in Lights."

The home is almost as astounding as its surroundings, boasting 10,500 square feet and is still originally furnished. The home was built in 1935 and was described as an English Renaissance home by its architect.

Birmingham Botanical Gardens

The largest public horticultural library in the nation can be found at Birmingham Botanical Gardens. As Alabama's most-visited free attraction, the gardens feature over 10,000 plants in its collections over the span of 67 acres. Its Japanese gardens include traditionally crafted structures and koi ponds. The gardens also feature two rose gardens in several outdoor sculptures, which may be found among its miles of paths.

Birdhouse Trail

In the downtown area of Monroeville, Alabama's Literary Capital, visitors may walk through Birdhouse Trail. The trail features custom designed birdhouses, created by area residents, to represent scenes from *To Kill a Mockingbird*.

The birdhouses have been featured in numerous media outlets, such as Southern Living, and photographs of the unique trail are a part of one of the Alabama Collections in the Library of Congress.

Legends and Folklore

The Civil War, with almost half a million casualties, was America's deadliest war. Most of this war was fought on southern soil, so it's no wonder that many consider areas of the South to be haunted. Added to the 4,000 Cherokees that didn't survive the Trail of Tears, the number of casualties in the South provide for quite a bit of mystery. From rumors of buried treasure, hauntings, curses, and blessings, you won't have to travel far to find a superstitious soul in Alabama. Some say it's just part of being Southern.

The Tragic Legend of Noccalula

Named after the beautiful daughter of a prominent Cherokee Indian chief, Noccalula Falls holds one of the state's most famous legends. Noccalula's father wished for her to marry a wealthy chief of a neighboring tribe. The chief had offered fine goods in exchange for the marriage, although Noccalula was madly in love with a man in her tribe who had little to nothing to offer in goods. Despite the pleas of the Indian beauty, her father banished his daughter's young love from the tribe. He then prepared a wedding with great festivities. Noccalula dressed in her wedding robe, but her grief could not allow her to wed another man.

Quietly, she crept away behind the noises of the rushing waterfall and the wedding festivities. She leaped off of the 90 foot waterfall to her death. Her grief-stricken father named the waterfall after his late beautiful daughter, and the name has since remained. According to legend, her ghost may still be seen, wandering the streams, looking for her only true love.

Today, the park honors Noccalula with a statue standing over the waterfall. Visitors may walk the gorge trail, which ends underneath and behind the falls, looking up at Black Creek. The park is also home to a pioneer village brought from Tennessee, a botanical garden with over 25,000 azaleas, a campground, a petting zoo, and miniature golf. There's also a small train for children and adults to enjoy the park with a narrated tour.

Bay Minette

In Bay Minette, it is rumored that a treasure of up to $70,000 was hidden by Spaniards almost 240 years ago and has yet to be found. In 1780, the Spaniards were being pursued by natives and buried the bounty, full of gold bars, in the area. It is also rumored that a separate, unidentified pirate treasure is buried around Bay Minette.

Somewhere near the railroad tracks between Atmore and Bay Minette lies another undiscovered treasure, according to legend. "Railroad Bill," Morris Slater, was a train robber in the area near the end of the 19th century. In his six year "career," none of the cash was ever recovered, and it is rumored to be buried in a cave. He was gunned down in 1896 and only left one clue, which was that he always stayed close to the railroad tracks between the two towns.

Perdido River

Near the Perdido River, another legend states that $100,000 in gold and silver coins are buried across multiple locations throughout the old ferry landing area (near where the current Highway 90 crosses the river). Until 1864, Henry Numez had been operating the ferry for almost 50 years.

After his death, the locals began to say that his treasure is buried in the area, possibly near his old homestead, where the ruins still remain. It is believed that none of it has ever been recovered. Although two small treasure caches have been found nearby, they have not been connected to the ferry operator's fortune. Another old ferry site, operated by the Numez family, is located in Seminole and is said to hold the family's treasure deep beneath the soil.

Pirate's Bounty

Fort Morgan was a popular spot for pirates in the 1800's. The pirates' treasures totaled millions in stolen coins and precious metals. Individual coins have been found that are believed to have been part of the pirates' treasures, but a large bounty has yet to be recovered. One pirate in particular, Jean LaFitte, is believed to have obtained over $10 million alone. His treasure is believed to be buried near Bayou LaBatre.

Florence

In Florence, there is believed to be a valuable treasure of all gold coins that formerly belonged to a local wealthy mill owner. C.E. Sharps, who according to legend, insisted that almost all payments to him be made in gold. Sharps owned a hundred acres across the street from the mill, and his nephew, Grady, frequently saw his uncle go into the woods with a bag and a shovel. Each time his uncle returned, he no longer had a bag.

Mr. Sharp was known to become violent, so out of fear, Grady never followed him into the woods. In 1899, C.E. Sharps drowned, along with his secret. Although his nephew was sure the fortune was buried among the 100 acres, the search was much too daunting for the tools of the era, and it is rumored to still be exactly where Sharps left it.

Shelby County

In Shelby County, another rumored buried treasure is said to have remained uncovered. A few miles north of Montevallo, there is said to be family silverware, currency, and other valuables still in the swamps. Before the arrival of General Wilson and the Union, slaves near Moores Cross Roads were ordered to bury the valuables from the Cunningham Plantation.

Carrollton Courthouse Legend

Most locals learned of the Carrollton courthouse in elementary school, and most love sharing the legend. The courthouse was burned down by a suspected Henry Wells. Henry was charged with and convicted of arson, burglary, attempted murder, and other charges. A mob formed outside the courthouse after the verdict was read, and demands were made that he be released into the mob.

Henry looked out of the courthouse window at the mob below, but a storm was approaching. Lightning struck him as he was glancing out of the window, and he fell to his death, leaving an image of his face to be permanently etched onto the glass. One hundred years later, and despite multiple efforts to remove the image, his face still remains in the window of the Carrollton courthouse.

Alabama Fast Facts

1. Matthew McConaughey and Sarah Jessica Parker filmed part of "Failure to Launch" at Cherokee Rock Village. McConaughey stayed at a camp ground in Cherokee County while filming.

2. Weiss Lake spills over into Georgia, but provides hydroelectric power to the state of Alabama.

3. In Montgomery, Dr. Luther Hill performed the Western Hemisphere's first open heart surgery in 1902.

4. Alabama produces more cast iron and steel pipe products than anywhere else in the world. It is the only

the state in the nation that is able to create these products with its own natural resources.

5. The nation's first 911 call was initiated from Haleyville in 1968.

6. Magnolia Springs is the only city in the U.S. to have all of its mail delivered by boat.

7. The first "Iron Bowl" between the University of Alabama and Auburn University was played on February 22, 1893.

8. The Unclaimed Baggage Center purchases lost luggage from airlines, stocked daily in a 40,000 square

foot warehouse in Scottsboro. As featured in *Vogue* and *The Wall Street Journal*, customers can purchase the unclaimed items at a discount.

9. Alabama was the first state to introduce Mardi Gras.

10. Willie Howard Mays, the famous baseball player, was a Westfield native born in 1931.

11, Jazz Pianist, Nat King Cole, was an Alabama native born in 1919.

12, Nuggets of gold are rumored to be found in the Little River.

Today, gold "hunting," whether by panning or using a metal detector, is allowed in many public access areas. Of course, hunters will need to seek permission on private land, but public areas in Talladega and Cleburn Counties may usually be searched after contacting the local forest ranger for more information on restrictions.

We hope this has provided you with many ideas for visiting and exploring the beautiful state of Alabama.

If you enjoyed this book or received value from it in any way, would you be kind enough to leave a review for this book on Amazon? I would be so grateful. Thank you!

Made in the USA
Middletown, DE
22 December 2016